# SPRING'S
# THIRD
# DAY

*Coming Soon From Planet Media Books*

*God Didn't Write THAT Book,*
A collection of poems by Judy Washbush,
Madison, Wisc.

# SPRING'S THIRD DAY

*Poems by*
## Laura Gross

*Edited with an introduction by*
## Dan Valenti

PLANET MEDIA BOOKS
In association with *Európolis Management*
Stockbridge, Massachusetts

SPRING'S THIRD DAY
Poems by Laura Gross, edited with an introduction by Dan Valenti
Copyright © 2010 by Laura Gross and Dan Valenti

Planet Media Books, founded by Dan Valenti in 2010, publishes new
works from new and established authors in a range of topics, including
poetry, spirituality, art, philosophy, politics, economics, cooking,
crafts, essays, nonfiction, and genre fiction. Emphasis is on creativity,
fresh thought, quality writing, and ideas of important merit. Planet
Media Books is an imprint of Planet Valenti www.planetvalenti.com in
association with Európolis Productions.

ISBN: 978-1-935534-457

*About the cover:*
The photo depicts a snowdrop, one of the first plants to make an
appearance in late winter/early spring. Snowdrops appear and blossom,
often when there is still snow on the ground. They are resilient, prolific
and utterly determined plants.

Printed and bound in the United States of America.
The Troy Book Makers • Troy, New York

*For Zachary*

# ACKNOWLEDGEMENTS

There are many people without whose love and guidance this project never would have been completed. Gratitude goes out to my parents, Thom and Sue, and sister Lisa, who encouraged me to write and to read other writers' words. For my teachers: Professor Valenti, who took me on as a private student and encouraged me to try out poetry; Professor London for a wonderful verse-writing seminar; and the English Departments at Berkshire Community College and Mount Holyoke College for supplying me with opportunities to write. For my primary school teachers for allowing me to always have a book in my hand: Mrs. Kearns, Mr. West, and Ms. Poopor. For a special, amazing, loving group of friends who have taught me gratitude and how to live one day at a time. For the two special men in my life: son Zachary and partner Paul. Finally for my relationship with a loving Creator, which grows stronger every day.

# Contents

Editor's Introduction . . . . . . . . . . xi
Author's Preface . . . . . . . . . . . . . 1

PART I: Damp Earth

Apparent Birth . . . . . . . . . . . . . . 5
A World without Adjectives . . . . . . . 6
Fading from Moonlight . . . . . . . . . . 8
Moon Monday . . . . . . . . . . . . . . 9
Awaken . . . . . . . . . . . . . . . . . . 10
A Tree in the Woods . . . . . . . . . . . 11
Dialog . . . . . . . . . . . . . . . . . . . 12
Solstice Emerging . . . . . . . . . . . . . 13
Constant Conclusions . . . . . . . . . . 14
Fox . . . . . . . . . . . . . . . . . . . . . 15
Gems of a Not-so-distant Past . . . . . . 16
Lullaby . . . . . . . . . . . . . . . . . . 17
Damp Earth and Stone . . . . . . . . . . 18
Owl-crossed Hugs . . . . . . . . . . . . 20
Ancient Dusk . . . . . . . . . . . . . . . 21
Spring's Third Day . . . . . . . . . . . . 22
To Kiss an Owl . . . . . . . . . . . . . . 23
"The Washover of Ho-hum" . . . . . . . 24
Now . . . . . . . . . . . . . . . . . . . . 26
Breathe . . . . . . . . . . . . . . . . . . 27
Grace . . . . . . . . . . . . . . . . . . . 28
Bluebird . . . . . . . . . . . . . . . . . . 29
Noise . . . . . . . . . . . . . . . . . . . 30
His / Hers . . . . . . . . . . . . . . . . . 31
Dreamer . . . . . . . . . . . . . . . . . . 32

## PART II: Stone

Tia . . . . . . . . . . . . . . . . . . . . 35
An Answer To Maya Angelou . . . . . . 36
With Gratitude To My First Love
    or Just Say 'No' To Smoking . . . . . . 38
Turned To Ash . . . . . . . . . . . . . 39
Priceless Gifts are Sewn in Beads . . . . . 40
Fellow Traveler . . . . . . . . . . . . . 42
A Girl's Most Treasured Moments . . . . 43
Glass Words . . . . . . . . . . . . . 44
Glass Words, a Toast . . . . . . . . . . 45
Illusion . . . . . . . . . . . . . . . . 46
Time Less . . . . . . . . . . . . . . . . 47
Old Stuff . . . . . . . . . . . . . . . . 48
Binding Time . . . . . . . . . . . . . 49
Private Snapshot, NY City Train . . . . . 50
Spectator: What a Battle is to a War . . . 52
Tantrum in C Minor . . . . . . . . . . 53
Soliloquy Speaks . . . . . . . . . . . . 54
Seemingly Small . . . . . . . . . . . . 55
Bottle . . . . . . . . . . . . . . . . . 56
New Boot . . . . . . . . . . . . . . . 57
Straight Line . . . . . . . . . . . . . 58
American (Parallelism) . . . . . . . . . 59

# EDITOR'S INTRODUCTION

Finding one's way as a writer involves entering through the narrow gate and walking a solitary path paved with words. Laura Gross decided to walk through that gate after an experience similar to mine. We both came alive as writers in college. In both cases, years of reading and scribbling came together in a "voila!" moment, and we realized, "Hey, this is my gift."

As I did back in the day, Laura signed up for all the writing and literature courses she could handle — and some she couldn't. We both made it a point to augment our explorations with a rigorous plan of independent self-study. Mine involved voraciously tearing through a massive and eclectic reading list and filling notebook after notebook with words. That work continues to this day. Then as now, the narrow gate requires total commitment, a prerequisite that separates dilettantes from artists.

❊   ❊   ❊

As so many of American authors did in the 19th and 20th centuries (Dreiser, Crane, Poe, Pound, Hemingway and so on), I broke in professionally as a newspaper journalist. Five years of daily deadlines and bylines later, I had learned all I could from the newspaper business and struck out on my own as a writer. I didn't want to be a dabbler or starving artist. I didn't want to bus tables by day so I could afford my syllables at night. I wanted to earn my entire keep from words. I dreamed big and got to work on the details. I rented an office so that monthly expenses would serve as the spur to exchange words for dollar bills. It worked out better than I could have planned.

While earning my bread and butter from writing, since 1977 I've taught in the English departments of LeMoyne College in Syracuse, N.Y. and Berkshire Community College in Pittsfield, Mass. I've taught courses in journalism, mass communications, expository writing, workshops in fiction and nonfiction, and composition I and II.

Composition has become my professorial specialty since 1992. I love Comp because it allows me to test my theories about writing. The classroom becomes a living laboratory. I work with a variety of students, most bent on utilitarian career paths such as nursing, business, and technology. Hardly any take my courses because they want to become writers. They take them because they are pre-requisites. On that I've never fooled myself. I help them achieve the three most important qualities in writing: clarity, concision, and unity.

✳    ✳    ✳

Poetry requires much of readers and audiences and hence has become irrelevant in the cultural wasteland of mainstream America. Poetry won't placate readers who prefer the surface and fear the bends that come from deep diving. This, of course, touches on the definition of poetry. I'll skip that, preferring to keep this introduction away from the "professorial" and the overly "left brained." As John Ciardi famously noted, it isn't so much "what" a poem means but "how" it means. Emily Dickinson said it best: She knew it was poetry when she felt as if the top of her head had exploded.

Laura Gross progressed remarkably over the course of our semester with her essays (Comp II, Summer 2008), but it was a lone poetry assignment that blew off the top of her head and mine. She said it was the first time she tried to write a serious, "adult" poem. She passed the course with an A, and, as usually happens with the march of countless students over the decades, I didn't think we'd work together again and maybe not see each other after that. I'm resigned to these partings — easy come, hard go.

Not long after the course ended, however, Laura contacted me. She said she wanted to be a writer, and asked if I would take her as a private student.

I've lost count of times people have told me that they "want to write a book" or "have thought about being a writer." When you ask about their writing experience, they mention that they wrote for the high school yearbook. When you ask about their current writing activity, they say they attend writers' groups meetings and authors' lectures.

Nice. I know I have a dabbler.

Laura and I met. Ten minutes into our discussion, I knew Laura wasn't interested in dabbling. Laura was in the process of finding her voice, figuratively and otherwise.

One way you can see that in these poems is her use of the first person — "the author taking up space in the world, becoming the 'I,'" as Laura puts it. Many of the poems use a "journey" as the main conceit, a device as old as the Old Testament and as new as texting. Many of the poems deal with nature or use natural landscapes and animals.

Laura knows which poems are her early ones, and maybe you can make a game of trying to find them yourself. The clues are there. I'll spill this much. You can find that first poem she wrote for me on page 56.

"The early poems," Laura says, "show the author as stuck and vanishing, while the later ones show the progression from helpless to walking with the sun illuminating the face. The use of nature as a healing element or a way to the soul is a theme that runs throughout my poetry." She finds in nature such "gems" as a heron flying overhead. This leads her into realms of discovery, of unfolding, of learning how to communicate.

You'll notice many poems deal with the seasons and changes of season. Laura uses time and its passage to show how she is "building her relationship with God," which is the essence of her "journey." As any story, one's spiritual biography takes place in and over time, and the quartet of seasons neatly submit to the job as chronological metaphors with divine significance. "Religion" as orthodoxy has no place here. Spirituality as self-illumination does.

In all of these poems, Laura has one subject: her relationship to God. She deals with human nature, not culture. Her topics include love, spirituality, and relationships. She doesn't take up social problems or political issues. In the process, she presents an extended definition of her self and identity.

Readers of this volume will have the excitement of literally watching and hearing a writer *in the process* of discovering her voice.

Let me conclude with the briefest of words about Planet Media Books. With this company, I intend to present new talent. In trying to find material to publish, I shall be a hungry lion prowling for a meal. The second book in Planet Media's New Writers' Series will be a book of poems by Judy Washbush from the great university town of Madison, Wisc. I hope you enjoy our maiden voyage and will share word of our endeavors with your friends.

— Dan Valenti
Aug. 12, 2010

# AUTHOR'S PREFACE

In the summer of 2008, I took an English composition class with Dan Valenti. One of the assignments toward the end of the semester was to write a poem. I had written poems in my wayward youth: sappy love poems to boys who would break my heart, responses to The Moody Blues' "Nights in White Satin," and angry poems promising anarchy and revolution. It was all youthful nonsense.

Professor Valenti encouraged me to continue writing. I did, and once the gate was opened, the words flowed. I liked that "first" poem, and what follows in this collection is my voice unfolding. In the past two years, I have been expressing myself through poetry and learning to trust that medium.

These poems explore the discovery of a writer's voice in concert with the natural world. It is through my time in nature — absorbing the sun and stars, floating in the water, synchronizing with the seasons, and listening to the calls of a pair of owls at dusk — that I have been able to allow the words to flow from my heart to the paper, and consequently, to allow another set of eyes to gaze upon those words.

This book is a tribute to all of my teachers, family and friends who support me, and to my Creator, whom I can lovingly call upon when I am alone.

— Laura Gross
May 4, 2010

# Part I

# Damp Earth

# APPARENT BIRTH

Pink blush upon my wintered cheeks,
pale blossoms emerge as countless weeks
of journeys toward an inner world
display secrets hidden in vines uncurled.

Whose visions cling to drops of dew,
that appear by magic in ample hues?
Be they princes, priests, or girls who dare
to speak a truth in song or prayer?

Our friends emerge within your grace
accepting love from spring's clear face.
In hope, in dreams, we spin our tale
of growth that bursts from behind the veil.

Sing to me, o child of frost,
of journeys fulfilled and darkness lost.
What is left for me to see?
Your vision God's pure victory.

Beckoned by your faithful birth,
Summer arrives to cherish its mirth.

# A WORLD WITHOUT ADJECTIVES

The summer came sliding,
scene after scene, all color
had matured past blossoms.

Autumn soon floated by
the trees filled with colors
that dropped to the ground and died.

Winter blustered from the north
unaware of the commotion
with its air like ice.

The spring arrived in June
long after it was due, yet
somehow just in time.

The year passed by devoid of frigidity,
warmth, swirling, and brilliance.
It just was as it is, here, now.

Without peaceful, soft, gentle, and brutal.
Without radiant, blustery, delicate, and luminous.
Without dark, exceptional, bright, and elusive.

The year passed –
It passed without elegant, graceful, dainty blossoms.
Month after month –
It passed without abundant, verdant, sumptuous foliage.
Week after week –
It passed without resplendent, vibrant, intriguing color.
Day after day –
It passed without sparkling, frosty, shiny snow.

The world turned.
The seasons revolved.
The year ended.
The new one began.
The world turned.
The seasons revolved.
The year ended.
The new one began.
The world turned.
The seasons revolved.
The year ended.
The new one began.
.........
...............
...........
............

# FADING FROM MOONLIGHT

When time stands still
and wind meets dawn
a small smile slips
from a child's soft mouth.

Young joy can be heard
in each blade of grass
and tears can be felt
in snow-like mist.

Touch wind, rain, and stars
with care and God's peace.
Fly to a dream land
on the back of an owl.

# MOON MONDAY

If I could be what I
wanted to be
the thought of a leaf
detached from a tree
I would swirl in river water
cool and bright
meander downstream
and take in the sights
by light of the moon
stretching my belief –
if I were a leaf.

# AWAKEN

A glance.
Pantyhose drying on a white cotton clothes line.
The edges of pumpkin stems, freshly chopped from the vine.

A look.
Towhee seated atop a frayed milkweed pod.
Fluorescent green lichen growing on an old oak tree.

A peek.
Bright red holly berries peeking out of crisp new snow.
Bumble bee hovering over new-fragrant cherry blossoms.

A glimpse.
Water crystals materializing on eyebrows in ocean mist.
The dance of candle flames on a checkered table cloth.

A moment.
Of seeing what never was, a tiny heart-shaped birthmark,
long eyelashes with glitter, peach fuzz, and burgundy.

A gaze.
At what is here, that just appeared
from behind closed eyes.

Awaken.
To spring peepers, pale stones, and the sun streaming
    through leaves
painting patterns on the deep rocky soil covered in vines.
To moments, to illumination, to facets of time.

# A TREE IN THE WOODS

Someone once asked,
Would a tree make a sound
if it falls alone?
Does sound need an ear
to makes itself known
or does it stand on its own?

Would birds in that tree
sing so sweetly if we weren't around?
Perhaps their songs would be sweeter
without our frail judgment.

Would that same tree
listen to my woes
or laugh at my blunders?

What is it with words
that they yearn to be heard?
Are they lost without us,
or is the opposite true?

# DIALOG

A low mumble of
insignificant noise
silently moves along the edge
of insignificant form.

Separating each strand
a different voice appears
to become a kind of its own
as petals form to leaves.

To pluck a petal off
the stem it clings to firm
is to gather a voice
from the cacophony of words.

Impossible to reattach
the petal torn from fronds
best to leave it where it stands
to gather up all time.

# SOLSTICE EMERGING

December moon
mirrors of light
shine.

Darkness on snow
winter's stillness
combine.

A journey,
autumn's equilibrium
align.

# CONSTANT CONCLUSIONS

On the last day of winter, with the sun setting, tucked
    behind blue-green mountains,
I set out to find a feather. Feet crunched on pearly white
    snow as I trudged through to the end
of the road. Next year I will do the same as I hope for
    robins to appear, as if by magic.

Longing for earthworms, toadstools, and lichen on rotted
    oak boughs, tiny red holly berries
peak from beneath the blanket of snow and crystals.
Does a season truly conclude, tucked away until the next
    year when the sun retreats and wild bear
fall asleep? Or is it always there, when the echoes of
    children sledding whisper in my ear?

White milkweed tufts swirl into a frigid mountain stream,
    shiny glass over smooth rocks, washing away
the last of winter's skirt. Soon crocuses will pop from the
    earth, as if pulled up by puppet strings, and I will wonder
    where the icicles will sleep, until the leaves, bright scarlet
    and gold, drop gently to the forest floor.

# FOX

Walk lightly.
She may be able to read your mind.
Perched alone on a silvery rock,
passing away the time.

Walk swiftly.
She may be able to sing sweet tunes.
Padding down a country road,
no clear sky in sight.

Walk silently.
She may be able to raise her voice.
Twirling through a forest of green,
tiny bluebirds in flight.

Walk calmly.
She may be able to lead the way.
Skipping through the rapids of ice water,
lightly on her feet.

# GEMS OF A NOT-SO-DISTANT PAST

Deep in the quiet of the
ancient past
discover diamonds
buried in ocean stillness.

Open eyes
soon to be drawn
closed delicately.
Seek emeralds
buried in hilltop vibrancy.

Find hearts
shut by words of lovers
hidden mysteriously.
Grasp rubies
buried in candy-scented clouds.

Still deep
in the quiet of the
ancient past
discover treasures
buried in soul's light.

# LULLABY

Go to sleep little one,
close your eyes with setting sun.
Safely dream beneath the leaves
swaying gently atop the trees.

Moon shines high, little one,
softly sparkling through window pane.
Venture forth within your dream
skipping down a meadowed lane.

When you wake, little one –
new and fresh to meet the sun –
dream your day among the trees
and shine with moonlight in your eyes.

# DAMP EARTH AND STONE

Sit at my feet
and I'll teach you what I know.
Let me draw you in with my scent
sweet, deep, damp earth and stone.

Deep oak tree roots and sycamore
wrap up the length of my spine.
Leaves drop into a murky pond,
making ripples in the cool water.

Sit at my feet
And I'll teach you what I know.
Let me draw you in with my scent
sweet, deep, damp earth and stone.

Silky rose petals and milkweed
entangled in my hair.
Wildflowers rustling as warm breezes
brush against white-tailed deer.

Sit at my feet
and I'll teach you what I know
Let me draw you in with my scent
sweet, deep, damp earth and stone.

I walk on a carpet of feathers and moss.
I dance in a field of flowers and snow.
I glide through a sky of clouds and globes.
I swim through an ocean of dreams and time.

I'll sit at your feet
and you'll teach me what you know.
Let me draw in your scent
light, love, green tendrils, and smoke.

# OWL-CROSSED HUGS

It was a movement so silent
not even the field mouse did hear.
Floating on light feathers and rose petals
they did commence to appear.

Dark velvet evening
blanketed with thick smoke and snow
came out of nowhere and nothing
then back to the arms of an ancient willow.

What was it that came clear
on that soft breezy night?
Was it the song of the whippoorwill
or the owl call that took flight?

Returning to sorrow
we bend and we break,
but in the arms of the feather
we peacefully awake.

# ANCIENT DUSK

Rider of the wind,
asking for what is not there to give
covered in dust and clouds,
leaden and filled with fear.

Spiral King, set in sand
as you move from behind the curtains,
do you see how that hidden look
has kept safe all secrets?

The weight of this dream
delays the movement of tired skin
through mud and vines
toward pinpricks of light beyond waking.

Illuminate the shadows,
and help me forgive it.
Teach me what you know.
I'll try to live it.

# SPRING'S THIRD DAY

A fire crackles
on spring's third day
as coldness seeps
into her womb.

Curled up in blankets
on spring's third day
away from wetness
and frosty rain.

Alone in thought
on spring's third day
with book in hand
and curled in chair.

The doorbell rings
on spring's third day
an instinct old.

He enters warmth.

# TO KISS AN OWL

I sat and talked
to the barred owls forever.
They sat and talked to me

with darkened eyes
that reflected soul
and feathers soft as sea.

We talked for hours
passing time,
waiting for clouds to flee.

We said goodbye
and they flew away,
in flight becoming free.

# "THE WASHOVER OF HO-HUM"

I look at the stars,
tiny lights glistening in deep eggplant sky
reflected in the frost

And then I forget.

I look at the birch tree
standing tall in a grove of baby pines,
bracing against the wind

And then I forget.

I look at the blue jay
perched on a white linen picket fence,
red berry in his beak

And then I forget.

I look at the sunrise,
colors plastered across the clear morning sky,
respondent in splendor

And then I forget.

I look at the infant's blue eyes,
young peachy skin, tiny fingers and toes,
nestled into her mother's breast

And then I forget.

I open my heart
to the magnificent brilliance that surrounds me
every moment that I am alive

And then I forget.

# NOW

Now snow, now rain, now wind, now frost –
'tis cold, until darkness leaves its earthly reign.
With visions of pure tenderness and hope
that spring will come forth this May, and until
her gift of blooms do rise, we sleep in cold
of winter's eyes. Those eyes do shine with ice.
When winter has her fill of us, she leaves
us to our joy, as blossoms bloom and birds
wake up and fill the skies with song. As streams
break free of Skadi's[1] clutch and flow due south
once more, we revel in the birth of spring
and dance so that new life may show.


[1] Norse Goddess of the Winter

# BREATHE

I breathe in God
with scent of roses.

I feel God in
grass sparkling
with dew of summer mornings.

God walks beside me
and brings me pleasure.

It is I who choose
to be a conveyor of torture.

# GRACE

A coyote crossed the road
the other day
and brought with him
my smile.

Two deer crossed my path
this very day
and brought with them
my joy.

Blue heron flies overhead
this lush moment
and brings with it
my awe.

God crosses my path
each day and hour
and brings with her
my soul.

# BLUEBIRD

There's a bluebird
sitting on my hammock
waiting for the grass to grow.

Little does he know
that tomorrow after dawn
the mower will cut it short.

His bright blue wings
and orange underbelly
strike against the trees.

He finally flies away
bored of the view
and running from my gaze.

Waiting for the grass to grow
little do I know.
Little do I know.

# NOISE

Silent – why must they always be silent? Walking on pine needles, strolling toward an ocean of deep dark blue water covered in sap, hearing footsteps on the waves, she listens to the sand. Silence, creeping silence, listening to silence through vines and dense forest of seashells, always smelling roses. Their scent blossoms on the first of May, always and never. Thorns grow later, after the waves cease their crash and leaves drop to the forest floor. What is left after everything dies? The stillness of the cool ocean floor, crusted in ice and prayer. Release your vows and sendforth gifts, an offering to the waves that will create a new song. Dance as silence retreats into dreams. Dream as dance returns to stillness.

# HIS / HERS

## HIS

Snowflake compartments silvery spike
downy individual not one alike
but who can say except as a statement of
god – architectural design faith
featured in a trade magazine,
the designer whose white facets, believed,
bring to bear from an infinitude of shape
even further ones, never before achieved.

## HERS

If I were to place a frame around joy,
it would be gold gilt, snow piles – fresh, white
and sparkling in the light from the streetlamp.
Snow dogs leaping through the powder, noses buried
into cold blue gloss. A sigh, a snort, another leap,
after fresh rabbit tracks. Now inside beside the fire,
ice melting from boots, forming puddles, they sleep,
content.

# DREAMER

Silver linings
purple clouds
who knows the dreamer
enveloped in shroud

Today tomorrow
without a past
the dreamer forsaken
the elements passed

Come back from the darkness
you chemists and thieves
and kneel to the dreamer
who never shall be.

# Part II

# Stone

# TIA

Tia Maria
sitting quietly
in the sunshine.
Tia, tia, tia

See me flying
arms outstretched
in the moonlight.
See me, see me, see me.

Hold me gently
eyes closed tight
in the darkness.
Hold me, hold me, hold me.

Tia see me.
Tia hold me.

# AN ANSWER TO MAYA ANGELOU

What could a mere poet be
who speaks of rivers
and rocks and trees

to a young girl
who might not believe
she is sturdy and free?

What if this poet told her
   *"Give birth again*
   *To the dream."²*

So this girl would know
how to touch the stars
when they appeared too far to reach.

If this poet rose,
and danced and sang
and prayed

would that young girl
see that she could
rock the world with her whispers,
unafraid?

To that dear poet
who pulled herself from beneath
and said to this young girl
it was all right to believe

to that rock
that river
that tree –
it is with tenderness and love
that I take root and grow,
to be happy
to be joyous
to be free.


[2] Maya Angelou, Inaugural Poem,
  20 January 1993

# WITH GRATITUDE TO MY FIRST LOVE
# or JUST SAY 'NO' TO SMOKING

Scramble.
Pick up lost pennies in the dirt on the side of the road.
Scratch.
Scrape your nails on pavement as the smoke from the
    tailpipe clears.
See.
Stare at the empty road and two shadows.
Stand.
Rise straight while wiping dust from eyes that saw
    something
        that did not exist yet did.

*You said I was pretty.*
*You said I was smart.*
*But the words you exhaled in smoke.*

Stretch.
Strain on tiptoes to see tendrils on a vine climbing the wall
revealing the lush garden inside, filled with words
that had yet to be believed.

*You said I was pretty.*
*You said I was smart.*
*But the words you exhaled extinguished my heart.*

# TURNED TO ASH

Backs turned,
an ancient mating call
rings out.

Fists fight through the air
competing with words
for the first blow.

"I love you,"
she says sweetly
as glass breaks into fragments.

"I love you,"
he says gently
as words crash into the mantle.

Backs turned
as marriage vows
are turned to ash.

# PRICELESS GIFTS ARE SEWN IN BEADS

HE
The simplest of looks
are well defined
in solitude
and words in kind.
ME

HE
Some far off place
we journey to
while behind his face
stream lakes of blue.
ME

HE
In timeless moments
we share a thought
priceless gifts
are sewn in beads.
ME

HE
What brought him near
seems an act of God
to find us amidst
many faces.
ME

HE
We never glimpse at paintings
to define pure color.
ME

# FELLOW TRAVELER

How else can it be said?
With words, a look, or a feather touch?
Fingertips to his temple,
taking away the burdens of the day.

What makes a person connect
with another traveler after passing
down the pebbled path alone
for stretches of time with only birds?

It could be said that the color
of eyes that sparkle on clear days
are enough to draw you into
the soft spoken words heard only in mist.

But when his blue eyes gazed
like crystals, she stopped her
saunter and took a breath.
How else can it be said?

# A GIRL'S MOST TREASURED MOMENTS

He showers me with flowers,
fragrant pink blossoms
faces upturned after evening dew.

He sprinkles gentle tenderness,
tiny kisses in the shape
of raindrops from a summer shower.

He presents silver baubles,
chocolate kisses and hearts
made from paper and lace.

What is it but his love
that's left for my eyes to see?

# GLASS WORDS

Flutes of liquid bubbling
froth touch and join
for infinite days.
I love you, they say
as glass touches glass.

Framed photographs hang
in mirrored hallways tucked
amidst roses and diamonds.
I like you, they say
as eyes reach for solace.

Words break as glass
when thrown against the mantle.
Splinters, shiny pieces on brick.
I hate you, they say
as fists find homes in dust.

Flutes of liquid bubbling
froth touch and join –
her parent's first joy.
We love you, they say
as glass touches glass.

# GLASS WORDS, A TOAST

Amid flutes of liquid bubbling
froth, hands touch and join
for infinite days and more imagined.
I love you, they say as
glass touches glass, a toast.

Framed photographs hang
in mirrored hallways, tucked
amid dried roses and diamonds.
I like you, they say as
eyes reach for solace lost long ago.

Words break as flying fluted glass
will when thrown against a mantle.
Splinters, shiny pieces on brick, as liquid tears.
I hate you, they say
as fists find homes in dust.

Flutes of liquid bubbling froth,
young hands touch and join –
both her parent's first joy, now another's.
We love you, they say
as glass touches glass, a toast.

## ILLUSION

No one will know it's there.
Illusive, seductive, white curtains billow,
and a smile with red lips appears from
beneath the crisp air.

No one will know she's here.
Ghostly apparition materializes out
of sand dunes. Clear jelly fish, pink baby toes
pop out from tears.

Someone will know who's near.
Candy eyes floating, rising from
moist earth, vines, roots wrapped
holding you here.

# TIME LESS

The sound of the clock
its marching tick
pushing me ahead
into my day.
It tells me to march,
that time passes
at an even pace.
Clock, tick tock
move move move
you are running out of time.
How I wish I could
take the batteries out
and stop the sound
that causes me harm,
stop the wrinkles
that begin to form
in lines of alarm.
But I am scared you see
to be ignorant
of the passing time,
and late for that final
dip in the sea.

# OLD STUFF

Suitcases packed
with bits of worn leather,
afrayed at the edge
soothed by the soft smell of butter.

Dragging behind
the canvas and plastic
what cannot be told –
wise stories by mystics.

They dream and tell
of the past as a rug
that rolls up when it dirties
to keep secrets snug.

When will they learn
that to clear up tomorrow
leave the suitcase behind
and with it fear and sorrow?

# BINDING TIME

Leather–bound words
from creators past
line up on mahogany
gathered in dust.

Who wrote such words
then copied them down
with black ink
that dripped
from a fountain pen?

Hunched over
a wooden desk as words
flowed through hands
and lived until ...

Now when eyes wander
over spines with gold
dates and names
only time can know

the smile that adorned
the cheeks of him
who thought that dream
we later read.

# PRIVATE SNAPSHOT, NY CITY TRAIN

Squares of light
of lives
flash.

Windows of time
of history
pass.

Strobed moments
lavish frames
flicker.

Leaving Grand Central
on a Thursday afternoon
catching glances of
friends never met
but histories shared.

Rocking cradle
filled with faces,
moments, days,
that do not return on the express.

Flickers of light
and smiles and hopes
and dreams cross tracks
with silence.

Flash
of lives
pass history.

# SPECTATOR: WHAT A BATTLE IS TO A WAR

Anticipation winds through a sea of multi-colored faces.
The crack of the gun startles bobbing heads
as cheers and screams infiltrate.
Names, numbers, and ranks blur.
Droplets of water spray into the air like a slur.
Heat rises from a massive tundra
sprinkling bodies across the defeated grass.
Skeletons run beneath the sweltering false sun,
diving into the grave that waits at the end,
that takes us all.
Silence, slow motions, and trophies tell
to mingle with ribbons and medals,
waiting for redemption to break the spell.

# TANTRUM IN C MINOR

I don't want to be good
I don't want to I don't want to.

I don't want to sacrifice
I don't want to be nice.

I don't want to think of you
I don't want to come rescue.

I don't want to be good
I don't want to I don't want to.

Stomp Spit Stew.
Screw You.

I don't want to be a lady
I don't want to act pretty.

I don't want to be nice
Stomp Spit Stew.
Screw you.

## SOLILOQUY SPEAKS

Who is to say,
to know,
to tell the meaning of truth?

Is anger the crackle of green logs
placed upon the hearth
or dried pine bows left alone in the forest?

Is it the breeze left in the wake
of the glass bottle that misses
a soft ear moments after tiny kisses?

Or is it the crash of ocean waves
when interrupted by a storm
after minding their own business?

If anger speaks, what does it say
if no one is there to hear it?

Or does it say nothing and slip
into the dark, damp moss, waiting,
waiting for the day?

Does it know the meaning of truth?
If it did, would we be there to hear it?

# SEEMINGLY SMALL

I
feel
small.

Wrapped
in
a
cocoon.

Ready
to
break
into
bits
of
insignificant
fluff.

But
truth
can
see

that
it
is
just
imagination
fooling
me.

## BOTTLE

I
feel
trapped
and want
to claw my way
out of the spiky cage
that jabs into my back as
the voices cackle in my ear
whispering sweet nothings to
me as I slip into the fear
and feel the tendrils
wrap around my
throat until I
am speech
less.

Bottle
falls
onto
ground
breaks
into
tiny
pieces
until
it
is
put back
together again.

## NEW BOOT

Hit
The
Pavement
Smooth curves, silky at my fingertips,
    running down a sleek back.

Win
The
Prize
Cold wooden spike joining the arch, falling to the toe.

Lose
Your
Self
Teeth join, hard tines forming a pattern, resting against skin.

Fade
Into
Black
Toe slips into tight point, arch settling on heel.

Vanished

## STRAIGHT LINE

Heel digging into sod, sinking into gooey earth.
An opening.

"Stand up straight,"

                                 Hide

"Walk confidently forward,"

                                 Run away

"Be all that you can be,"

                                 Marry

"Live your dreams,"

                                 Acquiesce

"Just try to run in those heels."

                                 Gottcha

## AMERICAN (PARALLELISM)

They tell you to run,
not walk,
run.
Dick and Jane run.
"Run, Dick, run."
We run on empty.
We run errands.
"America runs on Dunkin'."
Run for Senate, no
run for President.
"Run Run Rudolph" (but Grandma got run over by...)
"Who will I run to?" (Springsteen was born to).
Run the program, boot up your Mac,
run in your stockings, oh no –
just run to the store and put it on Visa
running up more debt (an act of patriotism).
"B-double E-double R-U-N beer run"
Now run from the cops, kiddies,
you are underage.
We run to stay healthy,
feet pound the pavement.
Don't you stop one single minute
5K (too fast for me).
10K (just under an hour).
26.2 (just over 5).
Run-on sentences
run on to the next line
always running we are from

place to place – from ourselves, from others,
teens run from parents
parents run from responsibility.
Jack ran up the hill, and Jill followed (of course).
Watch us go until we run out of steam and our
   defibrillator dies (battery ran out).
Just like Dick and Jane we run.
"Run Run Rudolph," we even push our pets,
just because Santa is running late
and Grandma ran out into the road.
They tell you to run,
not walk,
run.
Run away now, before I "run to you."

Planet Media Books, founded by Dan Valenti in 2010, publishes new works from new and established authors in a range of topics, including poetry, spirituality, art, philosophy, politics, economics, cooking, crafts, essays, nonfiction, and genre fiction. Emphasis is on creativity, fresh thought, quality writing, and ideas of important merit. Planet Media Books is an imprint of Planet Valenti www.planetvalenti.com in association with Európolis Productions.